Possible eff 12-team college football playoff

Supplement to:
Weighted Wins, A Better Approach

Ray D. Theis
Mark G. Terwilliger

In June 2021, a study committee was established to examine the feasibility of a 12-team playoff in college football. This news of a 12-team playoff was released shortly after the book "Determining the College Football Playoff: Weighted Wins – A Better Approach" addressed the problems with the current college football playoff system. Media reports seem to imply that the 12-team playoff is inevitable. The timing of the playoff is a big question mark as existing contracts would need to be renegotiated. This supplemental chapter is focused on addressing the apparent direction the College Football Playoff (CFP) steering committee is headed. From early reports, there appear to be two major concerns involved with a 12-team playoff: 1) selecting the teams, and 2) determining the bracket seeds. We will address both of these issues.

Some of the major disagreement with the existing 4-team playoff system deals with lack of transparency, conference protectionism, blueblood team recognition by the CFP selection committee, "group of five" exclusion, fluctuating criteria, and the "eye test" used by media having the effect of encouraging blowouts. The influence of the media and carryover value from year to year in poll rankings is obvious. As pointed out in the Weighted Wins book, in a 40-year study, only three preseason picks to win the college football championship actually won the championship. Yet in twelve years of the 40-year study, the team that won the national championship for a given year was picked to win it the next year.

This carryover information biases the true evaluative power of the polls. In a better playoff system, the problems mentioned above would need to be removed. Each year should begin with every team on the same level playing field. Weighted Wins does exactly that. In the next few pages, you will see the results of Weighted Wins in a 12-team bracket which can be compared to using the Bowl Championship Series (BCS) Formula to create a 12-team bracket. This analysis is provided for the years 2008-2013, the last six years of the BCS. After that, we compare the 2014-2019 results of WW and the CFP committee's selection. Because of the scheduling issues incurred by the Covid-19 pandemic, an analysis of 2020 is omitted due to incomplete data.

In the data and analysis provided in both the book and this supplemental chapter, we show how Power Five teams are given a higher preference over Group of Five teams. In the following tables, the conferences and its members of these two entities are listed. In the 12-team brackets that we present for the years 2008-2019, we highlight the Group of Five team names in red to help illustrate one of the differences between the Weighted Wins model and the BCS/CFP models. Independent teams are highlighted in green. At the end of the chapter, we present a summary and some final thoughts about what looms ahead if the 12-team playoff system is actually implemented.

POWER FIVE: Conferences and members				
ACC	**Big Ten**	**Big 12**	**Pac-12**	**SEC**
Boston College	Illinois	Baylor	Arizona	Alabama
Clemson	Indiana	Iowa State	Arizona State	Arkansas
Duke	Iowa	Kansas	California	Auburn
Florida State	Maryland	Kansas State	Colorado	Florida
Georgia Tech	Michigan	Missouri (pre-2012)	Oregon	Georgia
Louisville	Michigan State	Oklahoma	Oregon State	Kentucky
Miami (FL)	Minnesota	Oklahoma State	Stanford	LSU
North Carolina	Nebraska	TCU (since 2012)	UCLA	Mississippi
NC State	Northwestern	Texas	USC	Mississippi State
Pittsburgh	Ohio State	Texas Tech	Utah	Missouri (since 2012)
Syracuse	Penn State	West Virginia	Washington	South Carolina
Virginia	Purdue		Washington State	Tennessee
Virginia Tech	Rutgers			Texas A&M
Wake Forest	Wisconsin			Vanderbilt

GROUP OF FIVE: Conferences and members				
American	**Conference-USA**	**Mid-American**	**Mountain West**	**Sun Belt**
Central Florida	Charlotte	Akron	Air Force	Appalachian State
Cincinnati	FIU	Ball State	Boise State	Arkansas State
East Carolina	Florida Atlantic	Bowling Green	Colorado State	Coastal Carolina
Houston	Louisiana Tech	Buffalo	Fresno State	Georgia Southern
Memphis	Marshall	Central Michigan	Hawaii	Georgia State
Navy	Middle Tennessee	Eastern Michigan	Nevada	Louisiana
SMU	North Texas	Kent State	New Mexico	Louisiana–Monroe
South Florida	Old Dominion	Miami (OH)	San Diego State	South Alabama
Temple	Rice	Northern Illinois	San Jose State	Texas State
Tulane	Southern Miss	Ohio	TCU (pre-2012)	Troy
Tulsa	UAB	Toledo	UNLV	
	UTEP	Western Michigan	Utah State	
	UTSA		Wyoming	
	Western Kentucky			

In addition to these two groups, there are also seven schools that are independent, or do not belong to a conference: Army BYU Liberty New Mexico State Notre Dame UConn UMass

Comparing BCS and Weighted Wins 12-team Playoff Brackets: 2008

System	Power 5	Group Of 5	Group Of 5	Differing Teams: Bowl Game Result
BCS Model	9	3	#9 - Boise State #11 - TCU #12 - Cincinnati	#11 – TCU: WIN vs Boise State
WW Model	9	3	#5 – Boise State #10 – Cincinnati #12 – Ball State	#12 – Ball State: LOSS vs Tulsa

2008 12-team bracket based on BCS Standings

2008 12-team bracket based on Weighted Wins

Comparing BCS and Weighted Wins 12-team Playoff Brackets: 2009

System	Power 5	Group Of 5	Group Of 5	Differing Teams: Bowl Game Result
BCS Model	9	3	#3 – Cincinnati #4 – TCU #6 - Boise State	#11 – Virginia Tech: WIN vs Tennessee
WW Model	9	3	#3 – Cincinnati #5 – Boise State #6 - TCU	#12 – Penn State: WIN vs LSU

2009 12-team bracket based on BCS Standings

2009 12-team bracket based on Weighted Wins

Comparing BCS and Weighted Wins 12-team Playoff Brackets: 2010

System	Power 5	Group Of 5	Group Of 5	Differing Teams: Bowl Game Result
BCS Model	10	2	#3 - TCU #10 - Boise State	#8 – Arkansas: LOSS vs Ohio State
WW Model	9	3	#3 - TCU #9 – Boise State #10 – Nevada	#10 – Nevada: WIN vs Boston College

2010 12-team bracket based on BCS Standings

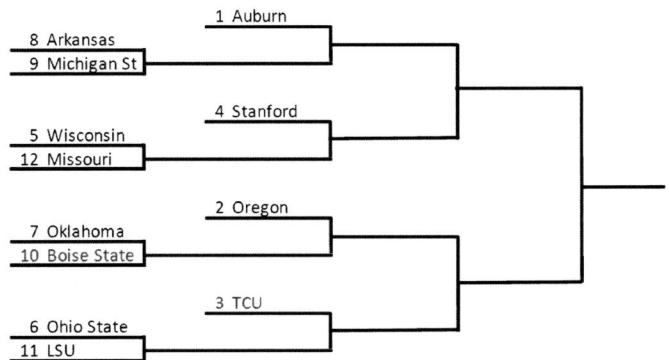

2010 12-team bracket based on Weighted Wins

Comparing BCS and Weighted Wins 12-team Playoff Brackets: 2011

System	Power 5	Group Of 5	Group Of 5	Differing Teams: Bowl Game Result
BCS Model	11	1	#7 - Boise State	#10 – Wisconsin: LOSS vs Oregon #12 – Baylor: WIN vs Washington
WW Model	10	2	#5 - Houston #7 – Boise State	#5 – Houston: WIN vs Penn State #10 – Michigan: WIN vs Virginia Tech

2011 12-team bracket based on BCS Standings

2011 12-team bracket based on Weighted Wins

Comparing BCS and Weighted Wins 12-team Playoff Brackets: 2012

System	Power 5	Group Of 5	Group Of 5	Differing Teams: Bowl Game Result
BCS Model	12	0	No teams	#12 – Florida State: WIN vs Northern Illinois
WW Model	12	0	No teams	#11 – Nebraska: LOSS vs Georgia

2012 12-team bracket based on BCS Standings

2012 12-team bracket based on Weighted Wins

Comparing BCS and Weighted Wins 12-team Playoff Brackets: 2013

System	Power 5	Group Of 5	Group Of 5	Differing Teams: Bowl Game Result
BCS Model	12	0	No teams	#11 – Oklahoma: WIN vs Alabama #12 – Clemson: WIN vs Ohio State
WW Model	11	1	#12 – C Florida	#8 – Arizona State: LOSS vs Texas Tech #12 – C Florida: WIN vs Baylor

2013 12-team bracket based on BCS Standings

2013 12-team bracket based on Weighted Wins

Comparing CFP and Weighted Wins 12-team Playoff Brackets: 2014

System	Power 5	Group Of 5	Group Of 5	Differing Teams: Bowl Game Result
CFP Model	12	0	No teams	#11 – Kansas State: LOSS vs UCLA #12 – Georgia Tech: WIN vs Mississippi St
WW Model	11	1	#8 – Boise State	#8 – Boise State: WIN vs Arizona State #11 – UCLA: WIN vs Kansas State

2014 12-team bracket based on CFP Rankings

2014 12-team bracket based on Weighted Wins

Comparing CFP and Weighted Wins 12-team Playoff Brackets: 2015

System	Power 5	Group Of 5	Group Of 5	Differing Teams: Bowl Game Result
CFP Model	12	0	No teams	#9 – Florida State: LOSS vs Houston #12 – Mississippi: WIN vs Oklahoma State
WW Model	11	1	#9 - Houston	#9 – Houston: WIN vs Florida State #10 – Northwestern: LOSS vs Tennessee

2015 12-team bracket based on CFP Rankings

2015 12-team bracket based on Weighted Wins

10

Comparing CFP and Weighted Wins 12-team Playoff Brackets: 2016

System	Power 5	Group Of 5	Group Of 5	Differing Teams: Bowl Game Result
CFP Model	12	0	No teams	#9 – USC: WIN vs Penn State #10 – Colorado: LOSS vs Oklahoma State #11 – Florida State: WIN vs Michigan #12 – Oklahoma State: WIN vs Colorado
WW Model	9	3	#4 – W Michigan #9 – S Florida #10 – Boise State	#4 – W Michigan: LOSS vs Wisconsin #9 – S Florida: WIN vs South Carolina #10 – Boise State: LOSS vs Baylor #12 – West Virginia: LOSS vs Miami (FL)

2016 12-team bracket based on CFP Rankings

2016 12-team bracket based on Weighted Wins

Comparing CFP and Weighted Wins 12-team Playoff Brackets: 2017

System	Power 5	Group Of 5	Group Of 5	Differing Teams: Bowl Game Result
CFP Model	11	1	#12 – C Florida	#7 Auburn: LOSS vs Central Florida
WW Model	11	1	#2 – C Florida	#12 – Notre Dame: WIN vs LSU

Comparing CFP and Weighted Wins 12-team Playoff Brackets: 2018

System	Power 5	Group Of 5	Group Of 5	Differing Teams: Bowl Game Result
CFP Model	11	1	#8 – C Florida	#9 – Washington: LOSS vs Ohio State #10 – Florida: WIN vs Michigan #11 – LSU: WIN vs Central Florida #12 – Penn State: LOSS vs Kentucky
WW Model	8	4	#4 – C Florida #9 – Fresno State #11 - Cincinnati #12 – App State	#9 – Fresno State: WIN vs Arizona State #10 – Washington State: WIN vs Iowa State #11 – Cincinnati: WIN vs Virginia Tech #12 – App State: WIN vs Middle Tenn State

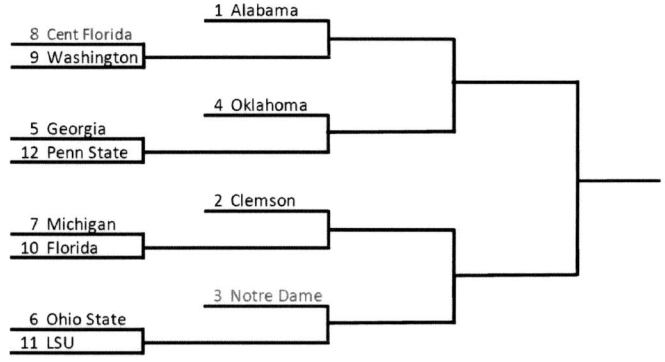

2018 12-team bracket based on CFP Rankings

2018 12-team bracket based on Weighted Wins

Comparing CFP and Weighted Wins 12-team Playoff Brackets: 2019

System	Power 5	Group Of 5	Group Of 5	Differing Teams: Bowl Game Result
CFP Model	12	0	No teams	#6 – Oregon: WIN vs Wisconsin #7 – Baylor: LOSS vs Georgia #9 – Florida: WIN vs Virginia #11 – Utah: LOSS vs Texas #12 – Auburn: LOSS vs Minnesota
WW Model	8	4	#4 – Memphis #6 – Boise State #7 – App State #12 - Cincinnati	#4 – Memphis: LOSS vs Penn State #6 – Boise State: LOSS vs Washington #7 – App State: WIN vs North Texas #10 – Notre Dame: WIN vs Iowa State #12 – Cincinnati: WIN vs Boston College

2019 12-team bracket based on CFP Rankings

2019 12-team bracket based on Weighted Wins

Summarizing the 12-Team Playoff Brackets

There were 32 different teams that would have participated in the 12-team playoffs from 2008-2013 using the BCS model. Employing the WW model, there would have been 38 different teams. Using the BCS standings, only three different teams from the Group of Five would have been represented. Using the Weighted Wins standings, seven different Group of Five teams would have been included in the 12-team brackets.

BCS Standings – 2008-2013: Number of appearances in the 12-team brackets

Team	App.	Team	App.	Team	App.	Team	App.
Alabama	5	S. Carolina	3	Michigan State	2	Iowa	1
Oregon	5	TCU	3	Missouri	2	Notre Dame	1
Boise State	4	Arkansas	2	Texas	2	Oklahoma State	1
LSU	4	Auburn	2	Virginia Tech	2	Penn State	1
Ohio State	4	Baylor	2	Wisconsin	2	Texas A&M	1
Oklahoma	4	Cincinnati	2	Clemson	1	Texas Tech	1
Stanford	4	Florida State	2	Georgia	1	USC	1
Florida	3	Kansas State	2	Georgia Tech	1	Utah	1

WW Standings – 2008-2013: Number of appearances in the 12-team brackets

Team	App.	Team	App.	Team	App.	Team	App.
Alabama	5	Cincinnati	2	Baylor	1	Nevada	1
Oregon	5	Kansas State	2	Central Florida	1	Notre Dame	1
Boise State	4	Michigan State	2	Florida State	1	Oklahoma State	1
LSU	4	Missouri	2	Georgia	1	Texas A&M	1
Ohio State	4	Penn State	2	Georgia Tech	1	Texas Tech	1
Stanford	4	TCU	2	Houston	1	USC	1
Florida	3	Texas	2	Iowa	1	Utah	1
Oklahoma	3	Arizona State	1	Michigan	1	Virginia Tech	1
S Carolina	3	Arkansas	1	Nebraska	1	Wisconsin	1
Auburn	2	Ball State	1				

2008-2013: Conference breakdown of playoff appearances

Conference	BCS Appearances (teams)	WW Appearances (teams)
SEC	21 (9)	20 (9)
Big 10	10 (5)	12 (7)
ACC	6 (4)	3 (3)
Big 12	14 (6)	12 (6)
Pac 12	11 (4)	12 (5)
Independents	1 (1)	1 (1)
Group of 5	9 (3)	12 (7)
TOTAL	**32 unique teams**	**38 unique teams**

Based on BCS standings, the three Group of Five teams (and their number of appearances) were Boise State (4), TCU (3), and Cincinnati (2). The seven teams qualifying for the WW brackets included Boise State (4), TCU (2), Cincinnati (2), Central Florida (1), Ball State (1), Nevada (1), and Houston (1).

Under the CFP model from 2014-2019, there were 32 unique teams that would have made a 12-team playoff. These teams are listed below, along with the number of times each team would have made the playoff based on CFP standings:

CFP Standings – 2014-2019: Number of appearances in the 12-team brackets

Team	App.	Team	App.	Team	App.	Team	App.
Ohio State	6	Wisconsin	3	Mississippi	2	Iowa	1
Alabama	5	Auburn	2	Notre Dame	2	Kansas State	1
Clemson	5	Baylor	2	Oregon	2	Miami (FL)	1
Oklahoma	5	Central Florida	2	TCU	2	Mississippi State	1
Penn State	4	Florida	2	USC	2	North Carolina	1
Florida State	3	LSU	2	Arizona	1	Oklahoma State	1
Georgia	3	Michigan	2	Colorado	1	Stanford	1
Washington	3	Michigan State	2	Georgia Tech	1	Utah	1

During the same six years from 2014-2019, the Weighted Wins model included 38 different teams that would have made the 12-team playoffs:

WW Standings – 2014-2019: Number of appearances in the 12-team brackets

Team	App.	Team	App.	Team	App.	Team	App.
Ohio State	6	Cincinnati	2	Fresno State	1	Northwestern	1
Alabama	5	Georgia	2	Georgia Tech	1	Oregon	1
Clemson	5	Michigan	2	Houston	1	South Florida	1
Oklahoma	5	Michigan State	2	Iowa	1	Stanford	1
Notre Dame	4	Mississippi	1	LSU	1	UCLA	1
Boise State	3	TCU	2	Memphis	1	USC	1
Penn State	3	Washington	2	Miami (FL)	1	West Virginia	1
Wisconsin	3	Arizona	1	Mississippi State	1	Washington St	1
Appalachian St	2	Baylor	1	North Carolina	1	West Michigan	1
Central Florida	2	Florida State	1				

2014-2019: Conference breakdown of playoff appearances

Conference	CFP Appearances (teams)	WW Appearances (teams)
SEC	17 (7)	10 (5)
Big 10	18 (6)	18 (7)
ACC	11 (5)	9 (5)
Big 12	11 (5)	9 (4)
Pac 12	11 (7)	8 (7)
Independents	2 (1)	4 (1)
Group of 5	2 (1)	14 (9)
TOTAL	**32 unique teams**	**38 unique teams**

Under the CFP system, Central Florida, appearing twice, was the only Group of Five team that earned a trip to the 12-team playoff. In the WW brackets, there were 14 appearances made by nine Group of Five teams, including Appalachian State (2), Boise State (3), Central Florida (2), Cincinnati (2), Fresno State (1), Houston (1), Memphis (1), South Florida (1), and Western Michigan (1).

Group of Five Top-12 WW Teams - Bowl Game Results: 2014-2019

We looked at bowl games during the CFP era involving the Group of Five (GF) teams. There were 14 bowl games with GF teams using the Weighted Wins system. The GF held a 7-5 edge over Power Five teams in addition to winning their only two bowl games against other GF teams. In the six years between 2014 and 2019, the CFP committee would have only invited one GF team to bowl games. Central Florida was the first team to crack that barrier. In 2017, WW had Central Florida #2 while the committee had them at #12. Alarmingly to the committee, Central Florida then went on to beat CFP #7 Auburn. Earlier, Auburn had defeated Alabama for the divisional title in the SEC West. In 2018, with a 25-game winning streak, the CFP committee gave Central Florida a #8 ranking.

Below, we list all Group of Five team bowl results during the first six years of the CFP era (2014-2019):

2014   Boise State defeated Arizona State

2015   Houston defeated Florida State

2016   Western Michigan lost to Wisconsin
South Florida defeated South Carolina
Boise State lost to Baylor

2017   Central Florida defeated Auburn (CFP #7)

2018   Fresno State defeated Arizona State
Appalachian State defeated Middle Tennessee State
Cincinnati defeated Virginia Tech
Central Florida lost to LSU

2019   Memphis lost to Penn State
Cincinnati defeated Boston College
Boise State lost to Washington
Appalachian State defeated North Texas

Comparing the Teams Left Out of the Other Model's Bracket

For each year of the brackets we shared, we presented the bowl game results for the teams that were left out of the other model's brackets. Another way to evaluate the effectiveness of a model is to examine how these "bubble" teams fared in their bowl games. From 2014-2019, teams in the CFP bracket but not in WW bracket went 9-9 in their bowl games. In that same time period, teams in the WW bracket but not in CFP bracket went 12-6 in their bowl games.

Pre-season Rankings: How do Group of Five Teams Fare?

At the beginning of the chapter, we mentioned one of the drawbacks of the current college football playoff selection system is that pre-season rankings make it nearly impossible for lower profile teams to ever reach the playoffs. This is especially true for most Group of Five teams. Below, we look at the pre-season rankings during the College Football Playoff era. Specifically, we examine where Group of Five teams rank in the top 25.

2014-2021: Group of Five Teams in Pre-Season Rankings		
Year	Teams	Pre-Season Rank
2014	No teams in top 25	---
2015	Boise State	#23
2016	Houston	#15
2017	South Florida	#17
2018	Central Florida, Boise State	#21, #22
2019	Central Florida	#17
2020	Central Florida, Cincinnati	#20, #21
2021	Coastal Carolina	#19

"Different criteria is applied when it is convenient. The results [of the season] have to matter… and they have to matter a lot. If the best thing you can say about Georgia is that they played Alabama really, really tough, that is not enough for me."

- Chris Fowler, ESPN analyst, reacts to Georgia not making the 2018 College Football Playoff

Weighted Wins is the Better Approach

The transparency and consistency of the CFP committee's criteria has been questioned repeatedly. The above quote from ESPN analyst Chris Fowler emphasizes the subjective nature of the committee's process. CFP executive director Bill Hancock, having to defend the transparency, on one occasion indicated that they could only reveal so much to protect the candor of the process. Since when does openness, truthfulness, frankness, or honesty need to be protected? All of the criteria spelled out on the website *weightedwins.com* and in the book titled "Determining the College Football Playoff – Weighted Wins a Better Approach" is completely transparent, does not fluctuate, and treats all teams exactly the same.

Another issue we have discussed is the exclusion of Group of Five teams from playoff consideration. As illustrated in both tables and narrative, the Group of Five was entirely excluded from the playoffs in every year of the CFP committee's work. Even in the 12-team proposed brackets, where only Central Florida made the CFP playoffs twice, Weighted Wins rewarded nine unique Group of Five with fourteen playoff opportunities for their earned resumes.

The pre-season ranking for the high-profile teams clearly presents an uneven playing field for The Group of Five teams. They are playing catch-up all year as the highest pre-season ranking for any Group of Five team from 2014-2021 was Houston at #16 in 2016. Conference protectionism is another issue that we clearly illustrated using charts and tables to highlight the unbalanced frequency of high-profile teams in the playoffs. The proposed 12-team brackets paint the same narrow picture compared to Weighted Wins. With Weighted Wins, the media influence with the "eye test" and "signature wins" falls on deaf ears. Weighted Wins, however, does not count margin of victory and it begins every team at the same point with zero wins when the season starts. No information from previous year is utilized.

Weighted Wins replaces the subjectivity of the CFP committee with a completely objective approach. The well-defined criteria do not fluctuate and is applied evenly to all teams. Weighted Wins' track record for isolating the teams with the best resumes has been outstanding. Prior to the bowl games, Weighted Wins has identified the eventual national champion 21 out of the last 40 years based on the team's resume. The following table shows the frequency of the final Weighted Wins standing for the eventual national champion.

Weighted Wins: 40 years of results*	
Standing	Frequency
#1	21
#2	9
#3	6
#4	4
#5	2
#6	1

* Notes:
- There are a total of 43 standings for the forty years since there were shared titles three times. In two of those years, the teams were #1 and #2 while in the third year, they were #1 and #3.
- In 1983, Miami (FL) was #5 in Weighted Wins behind Texas, Auburn, Nebraska, and Illinois heading into the bowl games. In the bowl games, Illinois and Texas lost, while Auburn won a close game with Michigan. At the same time, Miami beat Nebraska and jumped over Auburn for championship.
- In 1989, Miami (FL) was #5 in Weighted Wins behind Colorado, Notre Dame, Michigan, and Tennessee. In bowl games, Notre Dame beat Colorado, South Carolina beat Michigan, Tennessee had won its bowl game. But, since Miami had defeated Notre Dame in the regular season, it again won the national championship.
- In 2017, Alabama was #6 in Weighted Wins, which was the lowest rated WW resume to eventually win the national championship in our 40-year study. Alabama was granted the opportunity to play in the playoff over Wisconsin and Central Florida. Wisconsin had won the divisional title in Big Ten and Central Florida won the American Athletic Conference convincingly. Alabama did not win its division in the SEC. Apparently, the "eye test" was the all-powerful instrument. Clearly conference protectionism and name recognition are on full display!